Contents

Any words appearing in the text in bold, **like this**, are explained in the Glossary.

What does Earth look like from space?

The **planet** we live on is called Earth. From space, it looks like a giant, coloured ball. Earth is mostly blue because a lot of our planet is covered in water. These are the seas and oceans. The land is coloured brown and green and split up into **continents**. The North and South **Poles** are covered in white ice. Clouds drift around Earth.

This picture shows the planet Earth from space.

THE UNIVERSE

Earth

Revised and Updated

Stuart Clark

Heinemann
LIBRARY

www.heinemann.co.uk/library
Visit our website to find out more information about Heinemann Library books.

To order:
☎ Phone 44 (0) 1865 888066
🗎 Send a fax to 44 (0) 1865 314091
💻 Visit the Heinemann Bookshop at www.heinemann.co.uk/library to browse our catalogue and order online.

First published in Great Britain by Heinemann,
Halley Court, Jordan Hill, Oxford, OX2 8EJ, part of
Pearson Education.
Heinemann is a registered trademark of Pearson
Education Ltd.

Editorial: Nick Hunter and Rachel Howells
Design: Richard Parker and Manhattan Design
Illustrations: Art Construction
Picture Research: Mica Brancic
Production: Julie Carter

Originated by Modern Age
Printed and bound in China by Leo Paper Group

ISBN 9780431154688 (hardback)
11 10 09 08 07
10 9 8 7 6 5 4 3 2 1

ISBN 9780431154817 (paperback)
12 11 10 09 08
10 9 8 7 6 5 4 3 2 1

British Library Cataloguing in Publication Data
Clark, Stuart (Stuart G.)
Earth. - 2nd ed. - (The universe)
1. Earth - Juvenile literature
I. Title
525

A full catalogue record for this book is available from
the British Library.

Acknowledgements
The Publishers would like to thank the following for
permission to reproduce photographs: Getty Images
p. 9; NASA pp. 4, 5; NASA/Shuttle Mission Imagery p.
11; NASA, ESA, M. Robberto (Space Telescope Science
Institute/ESA) and the Hubble Space Telescope Orion
Treasury Project Team p. 19 Natural History Museum
p. 26; Science Photo Library pp. 10, 13, 14, 15, 16, 20,
23 (top and bottom), 24, 25, 27, 28; Still Pictures (Bill
O'Connor) p. 29; The Flight Collection p. 12.

Cover photograph reproduced with permission of
Science Photo Library/Mike Agliolo.

The publishers would like to thank Geza Gyuk of the
Adler Planetarium, Chicago, for his assistance in the
preparation of this book.

Every effort has been made to contact copyright
holders of any material reproduced in this book.
Any omissions will be rectified in subsequent
printings if notice is given to the publishers.

Our solar system

Earth is one of the eight planets that **orbit** the Sun. Earth is the third planet from the Sun. Mercury and Venus are both closer. Mars, Jupiter, Saturn, Uranus and Neptune are all further away. The Sun gives out light and warmth. The closer a planet is to the Sun, the hotter it will be. There are also millions of smaller objects, most only a few kilometres across that orbit the Sun. A few of these, the dwarf planets, are up to 2,000 kilometres (1,250 miles) across. Together, the Sun, the planets, and all the smaller objects are called the **solar system**.

This picture shows all eight planets of our solar system, from Mercury to Neptune. Earth is the third planet from the Sun.

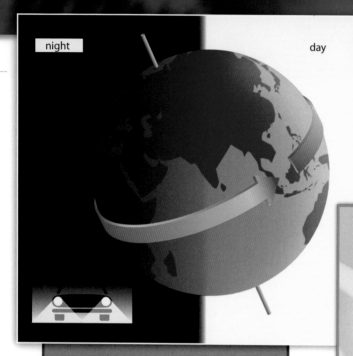

night

day

Because Earth is always spinning on its **axis**, while one side is facing the Sun (and has day) the other is in darkness (and has night).

What shape is Earth?

Earth is shaped like a ball. So are all the other **planets**. Some ancient people thought Earth was flat and if they travelled far enough towards the horizon, they would fall off the edge of the world! Anyone who watched a ship sail away knew this was not true. Instead of falling suddenly, the ship slowly disappeared below the horizon. This proves that Earth's surface slowly curves downwards, like the surface of a ball.

Day and night

Standing on Earth, it looks as if the Sun climbs in the sky in the morning, travels across the sky and drops below the **horizon** at night. In fact, the Sun does not actually move through space. Instead, Earth spins slowly, making it look as if everything moves across the sky. As Earth spins, it shows different sides to the Sun. For the side of Earth facing the Sun, it is daytime. At the same time on the other side of Earth, it is night. It takes 24 hours for Earth to spin around once.

Earth force

Earth has **gravity**. This is the force that keeps us on the ground. Gravity also stops the air we breathe from floating off into space. The **Moon** is caught in the gravity of Earth but is moving so fast that, instead of falling to Earth, it travels around it.

It takes about one month for the Moon to travel around our planet. During that time, the Moon always shows us the same face. Dark markings on the Moon are very old **lava** flows from **volcanic eruptions**.

While Earth moves around the Sun, the Moon moves around Earth. Both Earth and the Moon are spinning on their axis at the same time as this.

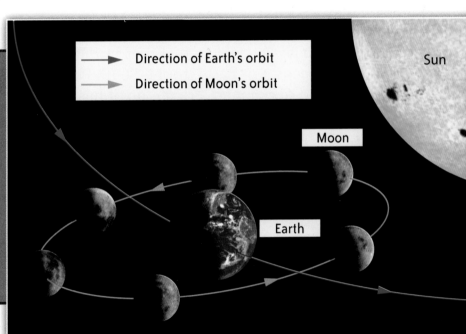

Direction of Earth's orbit
Direction of Moon's orbit

Sun

Moon

Earth

How was Earth named?

The name Earth comes from **Old English** and German. It was being used before the year 1150. It is the only planet in the **solar system** whose English name is not based on Greek and Roman **mythology**. To the Romans, the Earth goddess was called Tellus, meaning fertile soil. The Greeks called her Gaia.

Why does Earth have seasons?

Earth follows a circular path around the Sun called an **orbit**. All the other **planets** in the **solar system** also orbit the Sun. It takes Earth one year to travel all the way around its orbit. Depending on the Earth's position in its orbit around the Sun, Earth goes through four seasons: spring, summer, autumn and winter.

Going for a spin

As Earth moves through its orbit, it also spins on its **axis**. The axis is an imaginary line that runs from the North **Pole**, through the centre of Earth, to the South Pole. Earth's axis is tilted. Instead of pointing straight up, it has been knocked over to the side a little. When the North Pole is leaning towards the Sun, it is summer in the north.

Six months later, Earth has moved half way around its orbit and the North Pole is now leaning away from the Sun. When this happens, it is winter in the north. When the North Pole is leaning away from the Sun, the South Pole is leaning towards the Sun. So, when it is winter in the north, it is summer in the south.

The seasons change according to Earth's position in its orbit around the Sun.

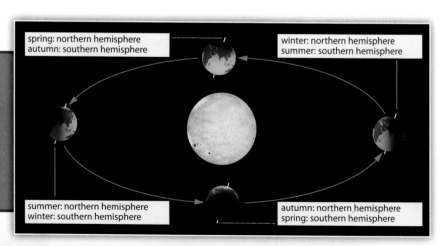

spring: northern hemisphere
autumn: southern hemisphere

winter: northern hemisphere
summer: southern hemisphere

summer: northern hemisphere
winter: southern hemisphere

autumn: northern hemisphere
spring: southern hemisphere

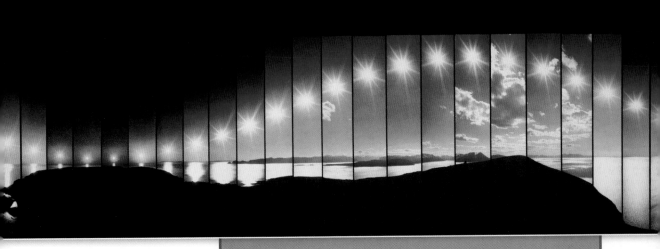

This series of photos were taken over a period of 24 hours, in Norway, near the Arctic Circle, during the summer. Even at midnight (sixth picture from the left) the Sun does not go below the horizon and therefore, there is no "night".

Night for six months

During the northern winter and autumn, the North Pole is tilted so far away from the Sun that the Sun never rises above the **horizon**. It is night there for six whole months. The same thing happens at the South Pole six months later. When it is spring and summer in the north, the Sun stays in the sky above the North Pole so it is daylight for six whole months. Again, this happens at the South Pole six months later, when it is spring and summer there.

Not all places on Earth have spring, summer, autumn and winter. The **equator** is an imaginary line around the middle of Earth, halfway between the North and South Poles. The area near the equator is known as the **tropics**. In the tropics, it is hot all the time. Some places have a wet season when it rains a lot. At other times of the year, it is very dry. Many deserts are found near the equator. This is where the temperatures are hottest and there is very little rain.

Why can we breathe on Earth?

Earth is covered with a thin blanket of **gases**, called the **atmosphere**. The special mixture of gases in Earth's atmosphere is called air. Although many other **planets** have their own atmospheres, no other planet in the **solar system** has an atmosphere with the mixture of gases we call air. So humans can breathe on Earth, but it would be impossible for us to breathe on the other planets. If astronauts land on other planets, they need to wear spacesuits.

The clouds we see in the sky are part of Earth's atmosphere. If you were standing at the top of one of these mountains in South America, the clouds and mist would be all around you.

Earth's atmosphere

The special gas in the air that we breathe is called oxygen. We need oxygen to change the food we eat into the energy we need to live. Nearly all living things need oxygen to stay alive. Fires need oxygen to burn, too. Not all our atmosphere is oxygen. Most of it is a gas called nitrogen. Nitrogen puts fires out. If there were more oxygen in our atmosphere and less nitrogen, fires would burn faster and spread more quickly.

The atmosphere is held around Earth by **gravity**. Some planets do not have atmospheres. This is because they are too small to make enough gravity to hold onto the gases. Instead, the gases float off into space.

Astronauts aboard the Space Shuttle *Discovery* recorded this rarely seen moment of a full **Moon** partially obscured by Earth's atmosphere.

How does Earth's atmosphere protect us?

The atmosphere does a lot more than just give us air to breathe. It acts like a blanket, keeping our planet warm. It also blocks out harmful **radiation** from space called cosmic rays. When astronauts spend a long time in space, their spacecraft must have a special room with very thick walls to protect them from cosmic rays. An alarm tells the astronauts when to take shelter because the number of cosmic rays has become dangerous. A special layer in our atmosphere, called the ozone layer, also blocks most of the **ultraviolet light** from the Sun. In small amounts, ultraviolet light will give you a suntan but large amounts can make people very ill and can cause skin cancer.

How high is the sky?

What we think of as the sky above our heads is actually Earth's **atmosphere**. The atmosphere stretches about 100 kilometres (about 60 miles) above the ground. Although that sounds like a lot, it is only about the distance a car travels in an hour. As you get higher up, the atmosphere becomes thinner. This means there are less **gases**, including oxygen, around you. It then gets more difficult to breathe.

This jet is high up in the atmosphere. At this height you can see how Earth's **horizon** curves.

The tallest mountain on Earth is Mount Everest. It rises almost 9 kilometres (almost 5.6 miles) into the sky. At the top of the mountain the air is so thin that most people who climb the mountain have to wear masks to give them extra oxygen so that they can breathe.

Flying above the clouds

Jet aircraft fly at about 10 kilometres (about 6 miles) above the ground. This is the highest that people can travel, unless they are astronauts going into space. Most clouds form between 2 kilometres (about 1 and a half miles) and 5 kilometres (about 3 miles) above the ground. There are many different types of cloud and scientists study them to help predict the weather.

Burn up

Entering Earth's atmosphere can make things burn up. Sometimes, bright darts of light shoot across the sky. These are called shooting stars but they are not really stars. They are tiny pieces of space dust coming towards Earth. They fly through space very quickly. When they hit the atmosphere they become very hot and burn up because of friction. Friction is what makes your hands warm when you rub them together.

This artwork shows how the Space Shuttle does not burn up when it re-enters the atmosphere because it is covered in heat-proof tiles.

Spacecraft

The lowest spacecraft **orbit** Earth at 515 kilometres (322 miles). Sometimes Earth's **gravity** pulls them down. Like shooting stars, they hit the atmosphere and burn up. In 2001, the Russians destroyed their old **space station**, called Mir, like this. They used a spacecraft to push it on to a **collision course** with Earth's atmosphere. The heat burnt up most of the space station but not all of it. It was so big that some of it survived and fell into the Pacific Ocean.

What is Earth's surface like?

Land and oceans cover Earth's surface. There are many different types of land. Some parts are covered with jungles, others with snow. There are rugged mountains and hot, sandy deserts.

Earth has all sorts of weather. Storms in the **tropics** have very strong winds and produce huge amounts of rain.

The oceans are very special. They are Earth's central heating system. They help warm up the cooler parts of the **planet**. In some houses, hot water is pumped around the radiators to keep the rooms warm. On Earth, warm water moves around the oceans, keeping some countries warmer than others.

The right distance from the Sun

Earth is very different from all the other planets in the **solar system**. It is the only one that has animals and plants living on it. This is because our planet is just the right distance from the Sun.

If Earth were closer to the Sun, it would be so hot that the water would boil away. If Earth were too far away from the Sun, it would be so cold that the oceans would freeze into solid ice. Without water, life on Earth would be impossible.

Factories and power stations that burn **fossil fuels** are adding to the pollution in our atmosphere.

Is Earth's climate changing?

Scientists are now very worried that Earth's **climate** is changing. For more than 20 years Earth has been getting hotter. Part of this change is natural. Throughout Earth's history temperatures have been changing slightly. However, some of the present change is being caused by pollution. This is waste **gas** from cars and factories. The pollution hangs in the **atmosphere** and acts like a blanket on a bed, keeping in heat. If we continue to cause air pollution, Earth will become too hot for us to live.

What is Earth made of?

Earth is made mostly of rocks. The rocks are made of many different **chemicals**. Scientists called **geologists** study rocks. When geologists know what a rock is made of, they can work out how it was formed. There are three different types of rock on Earth. These rocks make up the surface. The surface of Earth is called the **crust** and is usually between 10 and 50 kilometres (6 and 30 miles) thick. In some places under the oceans it can be much thinner.

Different layers

The first type of rock is called **igneous rock**. This makes up most of Earth's surface and was once **molten lava**. The lava **erupts** from **volcanoes** and then cools down to become rock. The second type of rock is called **sedimentary rock**. This is made of little bits of sand and other small pieces that drift to the bottom of the sea. As more bits fall on top, the tiny pieces are squashed together and become rock. The third type is called **metamorphic rock**. This is made from igneous or sedimentary rocks that have been squeezed or heated inside Earth and turned into different rocks.

You can see the different layers in this sedimentary rock along the coast of the Isle of Wight, UK.

Inside Earth

Geologists can use special equipment to listen to sounds travelling through Earth. It is a good way to discover far away **earthquakes** and **volcanic eruptions**. This process is called **seismology**. It also helps scientists discover what is inside Earth. When scientists first listened to the inside of Earth, they found that at the very centre of our **planet** is a large ball of metal, or core. It is mostly made of iron and nickel. At the surface of the ball the metal is molten, but near the centre the pressure is so great that it is solid.

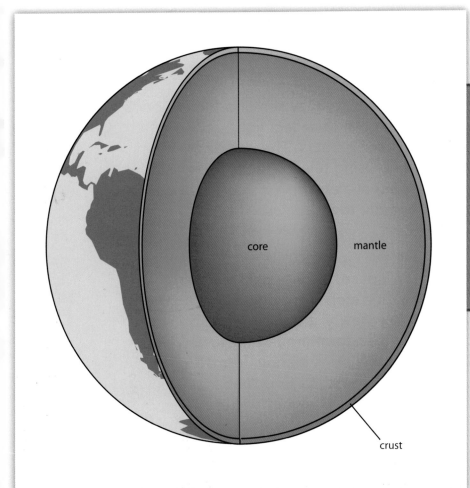

core

mantle

crust

Inside Earth there are different regions of rock (the crust and mantle) and metal (the core).

How was Earth made?

Geologists are very good at measuring the different types of **chemicals** that make up the rocks on Earth. By weighing the amount of each chemical inside a rock, scientists can measure how old it is. Using this method to find the oldest rocks on Earth, geologists have worked out that Earth is 4.5 billion years old. A big clue about how Earth was actually formed can be found in space.

Astronomers have worked out that the Sun is also 4.5 billion years old. This tells us that Earth, the Sun and all the **planets** formed at the same time.

Clouds in space

When astronomers look into space, they see enormous clouds of **gas** and dust. Some of the clouds reflect light, giving off beautiful red, yellow and green colours. The clouds are much bigger than planets or stars. Using telescopes to look inside them, astronomers can see that stars form inside these clouds. Planets must form inside them, too.

Star making

As the clouds float through space, **gravity** pulls parts of them closer together. This is the first step in making a star. As the gas is squeezed together by gravity, it heats up and becomes a star. Small clouds of dust then form around these very young stars. This is where astronomers think planets form. So, stars and planets form together, at the same time, and this is how scientists think our **solar system** was made.

Earth's **atmosphere** is made of:

Nitrogen **gas**	78 per cent
Oxygen gas	21 per cent
Argon gas	0.9 per cent
All other gases	0.1 per cent

The five longest rivers:

Nile	6,670 kilometres (4,145 miles)
Amazon	6,430 kilometres (4,000 miles)
Yangtze	6,300 kilometres (3,915 miles)
Mississippi	6,020 kilometres (3,741 miles)
Yenisei-Angara	5,540 kilometres (3,442 miles)

The Himalayan mountain range is the highest in the world. It is constantly covered in snow and nothing lives on the mountain peaks.

The five tallest mountains:

Mount Everest	8.8 kilometres (5.5 miles)
Godwin Austen (K2)	8.6 kilometres (5.4 miles)
Kanchenjunga	8.59 kilometres (5.33 miles)
Lhotse	8.5 kilometres (5.3 miles)
Makalu	8.5 kilometres (5.3 miles)

Glossary

asteroid small object orbiting the Sun. Some are just lumps of rock in space. Others are many kilometres wide.

astronomer scientist who studies space, planets and stars

atmosphere blanket of gas around a planet or moon

axis imaginary line that a planet spins around

bacteria tiny, basic life forms

chemical substance that everything is made up from

climate weather conditions

collision course about to hit or crash into something

continent very large piece of land on Earth. Europe is a continent.

crater large, bowl-shaped hole in the surface of a planet or moon caused by an asteroid crashing into it

crust outer layer of Earth – all the continents and oceans sit on the crust

earthquake when the surface of Earth moves suddenly

equator imaginary line around the middle of Earth

erupt burst out

evolve change over time

fossil fuel natural fuel such as coal, oil, and gas

gas substance like air

geologist scientist who studies rocks

gravity force that pulls all objects towards the surface of Earth, or any other planet, moon or star

horizon line where the land and the sky seem to meet

igneous rock rock made from lava

lava liquid rock that erupts from volcanoes

magma rocks that are so hot they are liquid and runny

mammal animal that gives birth to babies and feeds them with milk. Humans are mammals.

mass extinction when a type of animal dies out forever

metamorphic rock rock changed by heat or squeezing

molten something that has been melted

Moon, the natural satellite that orbits Earth. Astronauts first went there in 1969.

mythology old stories, told to explain how something came to be

Old English language people in England used to speak before the year 1150 – it is different from the English we speak now

orbit path one object takes around another

planet large object that orbits a star – Earth is a planet

Poles two points – one at each end of Earth's axis – the North Pole and the South Pole

radiation energy rays from the Sun

sedimentary rock rock made up over time from tiny bits

seismology special way of listening for, and studying, earthquakes

solar system all the planets, moons, asteroids, and comets around the Sun

space station large man-made object that orbits Earth – astronauts can live on it

tropics area of Earth around the equator

ultraviolet light special light that cannot be seen by humans. Ultraviolet light from the Sun causes skin to tan, and can cause cancer.

volcanic eruption active volcano that spills lava on to the Earth's surface

volcano opening in a planet's surface through which hot, liquid rock is thrown up

More books to read

Eyewitness Guides: Universe, Robin Kerrod (Dorling Kindersley, 2003)
Planet Earth, Deborah Chancellor (Kingfisher Books, 2006)
The Earth in Space, Peter D. Riley (Franklin Watts, 2003)

Index